Eye

Cover Image
Владимир Мельник, Dnipro, Ukraine (istock Master1305)

Eye

ISBN 978-1-763653-085

Walleah Press
South Launceston
Tasmania, Australia 7249

www.walleahpress.com.au
ralph.wessman@walleahpress.com.au

Eye

Julie Maclean

Contents

Margins

When the Light Fails

Exaggerating Perspective

Otway Fire Mother

The gully is numb today
eyes everywhere

as spirit winds
blow smoke fire

tangled atoms
into her dry hair

of wild casuarina
eucalyptus obliqua

Her belly soon fills
with baby echidna

a rare hooded plover
quolls

In her mouth
a caged platypus

swims from side to side
banging against her teeth

She spits it out as charcoal
like a lorikeet spitting seeds

while a lyre bird
mimics the frightened cries
of frogs—

Banjo
Growling
Striped Marsh
Spade-foot

too slow too late
to leap or crawl
from the boiling pools
of her sacred eyes

Solastalgia in the Mouth of the Great Vowel Shift

Going back to the word *zawn*   Are there any remains
  of that long drawled yawn   as jetsam

from the time they came in brigs and barques
  to be unstitched off the Otways?

What words did they use for splicing micro-granites
  in the unfolding of The Great Ocean Road?

It curdles the blood skimming over rough sleepers
  shipwrecked under neon in shop doorways

of a Melbourne street adrift in the *hummer druze*
  of 3am One carries a dog for a gun

The parish sprawls   in case you missed it
  We sweat for a ball click for a new wife

skid down the decay chain   flanked
  by rift margins sediments of keratin

  where if you listen you can hear the love call
of the huia sound fossil preserved by one man

Glossy yin black huia fanning its yang tail reel to
reel layered in waves fixed in crackle and hum

With words like Doomscrolling...

what century are we in? What time is it?
From across the closed world

you tell me you imagine your bookshelf
as a row of edible leaves.

I order my days as a Vermeer woman
with an apron—baking bread, taking time

to make the bed, the one I lie on
drowning in white noise I call The Hum.

The other day, I don't know which one,
I heard a call.

It was new to my garden.
I wanted to understand how Time

lodged itself in that black-capped turn
of a curious head.

It had one eye cocked giving me
the time of day before setting off on some

miraculous migration.
Or was it, like me, here to stay?

In some loose part of me I hoped
it would never end—this day,

this reckoning sky now open
to conversations with small things.

You climb the stairs an hour each day
calling it your solo trek to the top

of the mountain, praying
for enough oxygen to make your way down.

A Minute Past Dawn

I am up with the snails
They are usually grazing on
the dichondra
or lone strawberry   Sometimes
I find two entwined in a lovers' knot

This is when I have to stop
            and wonder at the ways we love
            and kill

I side-step this sweet scene
searching for the Moby of snails
its footprint planted firmly
in the door of my garden larder
where it leads the attack
on anything young, green, breathing,
            not moving too much

I try to imagine what it's like
to be Hindu or Buddhist
never killing so much as a fly
loving everything equally—
            this snail with its horned devilry
            periscoping every opportunity

or the butcher bird
spearing the fledgling from
its nest
Yes, impossible as it seems,
even this

Orchestra

Where I live there is no sharp flint to slice
the hide from a kangaroo for a winter coat.
No round bowl, ceramic smooth for cereal
with flavonoids, added iron. No coins
buried a metre down with the greening
face of a Roman Emperor.

Top soil is shaved off like dead skin, sold
to garden supplies for clean fill, a margin.
Generations failed in drought then flood
buy a raffle ticket for a meat tray
On Tuesday—Chicken Parma and a pot.

Beef cattle grazed this dry river bed.
The slater in my kitchen nibbled a
Cambrian leaf. That snail turned a
sliver of Devonian humus.

A swamp gum hosts a family of lorikeets.
It shades a baited hare, a fox sniffs opportunity.

The more we bury, the more he digs it up.
Or she.

I leave it fizzing above ground.
It takes on the look
of a mummified baby
until the bones bleach.

The wind plays it like strings of a harp

Bird of

When I couldn't conceive, he drew a lyrebird
        on our bedroom wall.
            Ordered me to colour her in.
                He had his peacock feathers on and winked as if
                I knew. I struggled in the charcoal
                    frame—such hard black lines.
                        That day he wore his Aztec
                            headdress as codpiece.
                                Seed pod gonads all the way
                                    down to the earth's core.
                                    My herringbone spine
                                    twisted to Kahlo
                                    at the things he
                                    made me do, sleep with
                                    portraits of dead men
                                    taking in their foetid
                                    breath, dusty company
                                    I'd been opened like a
                                    peony blood frilling in
                                    tendrils down my cherry
                                    blossom kimono. Dye
                                shot into rivulets
                            where the Amazon had run
                        so wet before. When it was
                    over I pulled my worn boots from
                the clod, spat venom into those
            spidery eyes, beat back sword grass from
        rainforest down the Gippsland road. Clouds
    were cobalt petals now. My pinks birthing
emerald and sapphire suns in the calico sky.

Murder in a Cathedral

Here is the how
the who of the dunnit

to the nest
in filament and stretch

barely breathing
choir quiet now

the where of
split trusses

and who did this
to my mouse-wren

the which
of the sacred clouds

gone missing
devil in the where

juice envy   spirit envy
hiding horns in the ruin

of rafters   raven
the pointless of the why

Wren in the Rubble

Is there a place on earth
a small corner without cats
or stray bullets where a girl can sit
on a square of carpet threadbare
staring at a small bird
scrutinising colour, curve, texture of the feather?

Could she try it on for size, geometry,
assess its capacity to ascend vertically
like an old Harrier Jet or pigeon from Damascus?

Along the Heysen Trail we were tailed by a Predator C—
white, winged.
We caught each other's eye until it lost its appetite and turned
away.

This girl sleeps with one eye open
soaring with drones and Super Hornets
night-fliers preened and shining
thin voice trilling in a wall of dust

Wait for me

Shar Pei

I sometimes hear
the strangled bark

of the neighbour's dog
and want to know

how he came to be so quiet
for such a muscular

suspicious creature —
that twisted skin

bred for fighting
This particular sound

makes me think of
how a war-torn mother

might sit her
broken children down

and try to tell them
without choking

Everything will be alright

Leopard Day

It's on a day like this
        I find a shrike with
        the crimped feet of the bird-dead
next to the kangaroo paw
I stand still in spite of fine drizzle
        soaking through my linen
        top   Pick it up by its fan tail
witness to the pathetic & true
Disappointed by its dull plumage
        I think of its lost song
The way it stops me
        in the ringing

Instinctively, I move into
my needled forest of she-oak
        camouflaged
My eyes
become black slits squinting
        against the splitting sun
lighting me up
My feet become soft paws
        soft-padding through the jungle
My tail can't help itself
This minute I forget who I am

        That the claws scuffing
backbones of skeleton leaves
scattering millipedes
        & hard bodies of primeval insect
will shake my morning's aria
        from the acacia   now ablaze

U plain

Every night when spring gets going
we sit outside in fold-up chairs
yours ripped from being left out in the weather
mine hanging in by a thread

You watch dragonflies like micro choppers
on some reconnaissance or other   I admire
the sass of lily buds   wattle birds in cirque
de soleil with kangaroo paw in a double act

I feed the fish that coil and flick in their rush
to be fed with their silly open-shut poppy gobs
You dead-head the odd drooped flower
pull a weed or two out of the path

We drink a few reds   knit the day together
You plain, Me purl   Your rows are always the same
I drop stitches   have to start again

You cast off   It starts to rain

Now That You've Left Me

for the desert
and a red rock
i thought i'd be afraid
listening for cars
on gravel
a door slamming shut
and I do watch out
for shadows
on white tiles
shivers of light
on the walls
mistake the head
of papyrus tossed
in the wind
for the head
of a bad man
but i'm listening more
to myself
sounding the rhythm
of each day
and what it gives
in solitude   in stillness
i'm not reaching
into the past
for some old love
but thinking of
sweet potato curry
seeds I have to plant
more than anything
a single chair
in my eyrie

my eye
to a galaxy in flux
the way it reinvents itself
the view I mean
and i'm surprised
to find i have no fear
and few regrets
except one
the fear of
your return

A Mustard Plant Will Remember a Harsh Word

by employing hormones
languages in bio mimicry
Lifters like ants and worms
know this
Colour forms in drifts
across the diaspora—
      Euphorbia, Gaura,
      blood rags of a Flanders poppy
How salvia blends
gives back as a sage friend
in soft bracts with outstretched arms
Water lilies cup clouds
become landing platforms
for pilgrim dragonflies

The Life of Trees and the Childless

I have a secret. I have stolen a plant
from my neighbour's garden—
the blue flowering one from South Africa
/rescued really, since she lets it wilt/
This must be like taking a child
from another land and bringing it home
to a glorious life of Boon and Plan Toys,
superhero pencil case and new lunch box,
sticks of carrot for your skin and teeth.
You shall have an iPad for your birthday
if we know the date.
If not, we'll make it up and celebrate
with cake and curry puffs as a treat,
stretch our lungs and blow out candles.

I will plant it with other blue flowers
that have not been stolen but foraged
or purchased. In this way it should feel
more comfortable, less alone, and give
off pleasant scents and signals to attract
bees and deter small flies
that want to suck the life out of it.
I shall water often at the start then foster
resilience as it becomes established.
I am following what Jekyll says —
plant in blocks of colour or drifts
as in a Turner where the light
is always there. /At times his strokes
seem so heavy-handed—he was a bit mad/
though plenty of yellow—and the light,
light pushing through. A glimmer at least.

Absolute Zero

You often watch me as I go to the wild place
where winter beetles roll
the sun across the sky and away

I'm snipping wing-tips of pin-cushion hakea
What you don't see is
black-striped bees coming for me

Some are disappearing
through a secret door into the belly
of the bluestone plinth

But my head is alive with news of the boy
wedged between honeycomb wall and limestone

A subversive chill mingles
with his calcium as the father excavates
an extra space to plant a bay

finding instead his DNA petrified
in the twisted frame of his lost son
draped in blue and white striped summer cotton

Bees rise from the body as tears
        filling his father's empty hives

Leaf Life

if only it were enough
to carry a leaf aloft

to wave the word
along the long leaf road

to wear a headpiece of leaves
that says do not quit

this place without grace
without leaves

weave them into the fabric
of your heart, do not begin

without them, be driven
by the gentle engine of a leaf

Salt Sweeps

Sirenia at the Lido

I'm not on drugs
or
dancing in the moonlight when
the shape of the water shifts under me
Dugongs are breaking
in the shallows
Nothing like Bboys, Bgirls—
rappers   hip-hoppers
No jackhammers   freezes   hand-hops
airflares   headspins   kip-ups
no caps back to front
only cows
of the sea
mild and slow

Unglamorous beasts in unsung rhythm
in sync they graze fields of grass among the mangroves
minding their own business

This trio performs the show of the year
under a nightclub sky   for me
But I have one question o solé mio

Where do the old tired and quiet go to die?

Promontory Song to Hymen

Boulders settle here without licence
        lobes itchy with lichen
one in the shape of a whale
        without a tongue

Avenues of honey myrtle
        pose as bridal veils for hopefuls
in spring

        Fifty metres down
        remnant seals   fins of dolphins
show and clasp in the refuge of cleft rock
        hymns click   high-pitched
beyond ear   and receding

On a tidal river brackish
        with the fallen   ghost children
        make patterns in sand with twigs
tracking thylacine   across the lachrymal divide

Sun spirals down   haloes crown
        on banksia bracts   occult
                in this melon light
hanging their harps up
                        on marsupials
coiled and small
        this dry childless night

41 North 50 West

This is the imprecise location
where the Titanic was strafed
by an AK 47 in 1912 and slumped
where at 4.15pm on a liner

bound for an empire I looked out
from the balcony for a sign of Rose and Jack Dawson
and in leapt two dolphins
        one for each eye

        /They circled with other motes in there
        gathering like great whites
        to witness my reaction to the tragedy/

I checked the radar for icebergs. It was spring.
They were splintering south
but the sea was empty while my eyes were alive
with cheery mammals nudging me to tears
so they could slip out to try the buffet:
European cheese   Rocquefort and Brie

Precisely one century later a Bengal tiger—
Richard Parker   jumped right into my lap in Ang
Lee's Life of Pi   3D so terrifying my eye dolphins
seemed like they'd come for a play

Dolphins and whales confounded Aristotle
beaching themselves in 350 BC
glittering pelts dried black along shores
of Greek islands like Kos
like the sunburst skins of fugitive children today

Winged and Killing after Catullus

Some birds are hard to love
the blue heron   currawongs
wodjaloks with crimson wattles
growling from my balcony
                              like dogs

I've seen one machete the soft neck
of a female in spring
then poke flimsy throats
of virgin grevillea
in a rhapsody of blood and foreplay

The driven
drop nerve agents   on children
hurl acid in a woman's face
                              on a Sydney Street

and that three-year-old washed up
                                        on the beach
his tucked-in shirt lifted
ever so gently by the ripple of an incoming tide
so he looked for a moment   full of breath
                              utterly alive

Lizard Life

You marvel at the slumped devils
basking in the glow
of the crescent moons of the
      Galapagos
Marine iguana slouch à la Kerry Packer
in a swivel chair

They graze the green on reefs
      Browse on seaweed
or breast stroke to the ocean floor
      Sometimes diving
        as Olympians

Holding breath they look for pearls
      Faustian spawn
grow snappy teeth and spit out salt

      They will not eat you
El Niño is good news for scavengers
      like these   When algae dies
Sally Lightfoot sidesteps in
      Dainty crab a splash of Cezanne red
against Picasso grey

      Rock canvas
of evolving traits   Bones shrink
when rain stops   Snouts slim down
      for poking into small crevices

They shrivel on dry land Pelts of roadkill
      the Antipodean way

Emoto's Theory of Rock Pool Phenomena

The water remembered me today
its nervous system alive to my approach
from the surf beach past the usual cave reeking of dead
mermaids and visitors' piss

Receptor panels alert to blue
composed molecules   as if for a chamber recital
         aerobic as a prelude

         I could feel the salty cello reverberating
         untangling my distracted helix
         exhausted from caring for the sick and dying
         worrying about endings and beginnings

It sent me a love signal at just the right frequency

         The sky wasn't especially clear that day
         but reedy weed broken shells
         and a crab claw lay in a planetary scattering
         of celestial harmony

Chaos came in the background noise—
         blondes in seal suits whooping in the spume
         black holes colliding by the gazillion

I knew if I didn't pay attention this moment would spoil
go out of tune in a minute
It held me in its thrall this pool I'd picked my way around
and through every season for aeons
without so much   as a rogue thought
Hell at low tide   that black snapping dog

Piffing Yonnies into the Post-Industrial

The summit used to be all   but now   scuffed
runners   a notebook   and when no one's

looking   I gobble   from a can of cold beans
nestling in the sprawl   of a dry creek bed

picking out constellations on a Skyview app   as a
lone satellite   drawls by   in its chilly orbit

It sends out   coded murmurings   to night birds,
marsupials

In glass cities   red eyes on night watch   don't own them
Tame hearts   drunk on the earthbound cute

colouring in   joining dots   loose scree forming
at their feet

       Who can tell a possum from a Pikachu?

There'll come a time   the word *quoll*   is not heard
any more   as *cassowary*   *swift parrot*

settle into sediment   with *thylacine*   tossed in
moraines   smoothing

not worth bottling   like a man's blood
   In Net slang   TQT   this is quoted for truth

children cannot name   a leaf on a plate   a tree
      collective noun for anything

Found flat stones   in full swim   thought bubbles
   skimming shallows   monosyllables
     s p l a s h e d   in monochrome

Shark Baby Hallelujah

Lamb-boy with wings   I want to keep you
but not as a tooth sculpture on a plinth
posing before vintage bookery or rusting
among machinery of men
where simple stone is gripped
with such a root system
such grunt and muscularity

You and I   stitched together instead
as voile   the ease and sheerness of you
in symbiosis

I harbour you, my sacred parasite
under this canopy of stellar activity
and sonar

You are my pillow-ticking chrysalis
      I finger each of your vertebrae
        through the flesh carapace
         of my doming womb
         You are my abacus
         and I am counting down
      Slick grub
   your backbone positively gleams
in your special upholstery

Salt Wind Salt War

As cumuli mass in platoons
over Tribulation
they strike me as bones of a whale

but what they are for real
are supplicant fingers of pure palm
tumbled by the muscle of a cyclone

Fronds shudder and click
like pelican beaks

in times of famine
tearing breasts open
        to feed chicks
        straight from the heart   pure blood
        leaving stigmata
on parchment feather

In drought they quietly
        pile the dead for shade
        roll eggs into death cairns
        little abortions cloud about
skirts of Kati Thanda   Lake Eyre

not here   where death comes in all weathers
peace time rare as ambergris

Bullet Winds

are bastards in this otherwise nirvana
Stretched along the gunwales, mainsail tight
relaxing into Chapter Three, a sudden gust
whips your Prada glasses off   Hawaiian scenes
on beach towels are manta rays   airborne

A passing turtle pulls her head in, closes shop
accustomed to a less aggressive approach
from the barnacled alpha that comes upon her quietly
at low tide in spring, green algae
                    streaming off his nubby keel

After summer volunteers rake the bed   avoiding
stone fish and cone shells   ordinary-looking
marine life that could kill
                    with a well-aimed barb and sting

Dive teams retrieve our crap
                    Overpriced,
                    last year's trendy
                    Let's all go see
                    the Barrier Reef
                    while we can
                    sunk-sodden flotsam
                                        replaceable crap

Loggerhead

Slicing through a safe passage
out of Hook Island
our white sloop with the sharp sprit
races for home
when a spaceship is sighted
from the helm bobbing
on the anxious surface

She's missed James Cook
by a hundred years head tucked in
to avoid collateral damage

We power on with the jib yawning
while a hundred metres back
an old head comes out of its shell
with the eyes of an old soul
raising an ancient eyebrow

Old Man off the Solstice

Surely
He's come to die
Under the palms
Among the pumice and half- moon coconut shells
        /Nembutal in his bag/
Or to find love between the flags
                Tide in Tide out
It's hard to tell
His dreams the dreams
Of the young
He wears Lycra
With a red flash
Lightning strike barely covering his pride
His shame
There's a penguin
On his beach towel from Fiji
He is reading Lee Childs
Learning how to murder five ways
How to swing a baseball bat
        /for maximum impact/
He is gazing out to the horizon
Killing time

He Makes a Difficult Choice and Says

One wants to be free to choose the death
unlike Heraclitus devoured by dogs
One wants to be free to choose
whether to be stabbed by nine friends
high on life in a Brisbane flat, or not
when to invite the eagle to drop
a tortoise onto one's head
mistaking it for a rock
as in the case of Aeschylus
One wants to be free to choose
when the death is at the appropriate time
not taking a hike alone
to the Fluted Cape on Bruny Island
slipping over the edge, aged 27,
never to be seen again
One wants to wear a tee   *ageing disgracefully*
but not if it means stringing oneself up
by one's belt to the bedroom door—
a poor prognosis hanging in the air
One does not want
to be beaten to death by a Bible
during a healing ceremony gone wrong
or be Mary the elephant hanged by the neck
on an industrial crane for killing her trainer—
fifty cents a look
Beethoven's 9th might be nice
a glass of gin and freshly squeezed
with my Nembutal   please

And the Rivers Run with Antibodies

in blood-blue arteries of artless flight
        and gather
                egrets meet and feed
in shallow
                shadow   peace
        and blue

on sand bars   ochre red
        beaks and birds feed as cells

                cancer breeds like birds
birds in shallows   deep
        eat and eat

feed in blood
        in blood-blue river   river of blood
and bird

they nod
        and nod
                slash the cancer down
eat the fish
        the cancer fish
                fish and cancer feed

blue arteries collapse
        fold as egrets feed
                on drought
                        rare treat
                                and cancer tides

Little Picture

Today I must construct myself
Tomorrow the sky will be static
                              without birds
There are rock pools where I go
purple patches   greens
Uncle Toby's factory
closed a grin on every face
on every fish   I hope

I will snorkel a reef
look both ways to find you
in a straw hat   striped shirt
                           blonde smile

Reels of film will spill out
onto clouds bruised with storm fronts

Where I go   reaching for
the lucky seven   the indigo
there's a photo of us eighteen
                           smoking cigarettes

a sketchbook in acrylics
celluloid faces in the drape
                           of a cloth

One more draft and I swear I'll
go   in the shadow of a witness
                           without words

Margins

Quietude

In the absence
of the roar
I could hear
atoms in ozone
colliding as rain clouds
rearranged themselves
I could hear
moss nibbling
on a piece of scoria
the gentle purring
of a wolf spider
in the far corner
of a bedroom
in another
hemisphere
A faint thrum
intruding
upon the dumb
circularity
of our lives

How Deep is Your Love

I grow shallow in the breadth of your thoughts
heavy under the weight of your slow breathing

Small children wrap plastic bags around your leaves
to prove you are alive   You are alone

and with your unseen ears   have witnessed
the shelling of a thousand wars   a hundred and fifty

years in some man's land like a neutral country glowing
in the middle of a darkening union   now showing signs

Fast growing wreaths of roads and smoke
compete with weakening buttresses   your cathedral sags

Perhaps you're done as the Children's Tree   fenced off
now with aerials like stick-men   wrapped around

each other for succour   glad of the rains
pitting hardening skin at your feet

When my son was seven I asked him to paint you
He split the canvas with a perfectly straight horizon

Underground roots as arteries
pumped blood wide across a black universe

Above ground leaves as green clouds
pillowed in a breathless sky

True Bird Nature of a Tree

it leads a double life
as basilica, strangling vine
arms out of reach
of the human hand

vaults
      fit for a figbird
towering tree
      fit for a bowerbird
children's tree
      fit for a catbird
banyan tree
      fit for a fruit dove
medicine tree
      fit for a wompoo
rooty tree
      fit for a crow
oldest tree
      fit for a
      sparrow
      cuckoo shrike
      currawong
      pigeon
      wattle bird
      lorikeet
      ladybird

signature bird   wingspan of a football field

Homeless Woman Hallucinates Walking Past the Garden Palace in 1879

There are days even the sky seems green
I wear a summer one decorated with magnolia

sip opium from a vial under the fig
Perched on one end of my hat   ridiculously big
but practical a New Holland honeyeater is waiting

for a friend, bats drip in the mango
But my nails grow long and the dress I wear today
is a lawn trimmed with hand-hewn sandstone

Joe Banks strolls by deep in stigmas and stamens
Turrets of this castle are my eyes on fire
My brain the dome   It slows

I list the beauties
seek out categories   steal Latin names

See how pink-cupped water lilies—Nymphaea
mirror my green breasts
the way my bare toes ripple the green sky lake

There's a portal to the sea   a lone dragonfly
comes in as a drone from a future world and takes up
residence on my north face
                                        I let it stay

Not Swan Lake

Between naps
and a good book
on the Matilda
the verges are
green monotone

We should be
thankful for the wet
I know

Then the reminder
stubble
from burn-off or patch fire
relieved by a pair
of brolgas
They dance and nibble
like lovers

Then sudden lift off
in a pas de deux
Crane necks
in an arc
finely tuned
grace of needle bone
He and She
embroider the sky
in ballet tapestry nouveau

Festa Junina

Drowned man,
you lured me into your voice
I was tempted by your cheap guitar,
catfish shoes.

You held me between diamond teeth,
hiding your river life
under a fedora and a white suit.
I didn't see the opening
in your head breathing your boto lies until later.
That night I found you lounging
like a manatee

on the stone wall outside my house
keen to show me your talisman.
It was human.

I looked the other way,
shut legs and ventricles against you.

In shell breaths I sang like a Rhine siren
I like you alright but you smell all wrong.

      It was the winter solstice.
      Ocean turning on itself in the whip
      of a south westerly. I turned from you.
See, I am leaning south

You turn on a fin, slide back to your sun.
      I take familiar steps towards soft spring.

Dogged

When I returned
the garden was a riot
of bickering dogs

In the kitchen
you were baking a cake
and showed me your new breasts
where a man's chest had been—
          bumpy, toned

          There were food stains
on your Bali-blue shirt
I scratched at soft flakes
which came off easily
on the firm rise of
          silicone

          Survivors of the fire
          had set up camp next door

Some had plants
          in wrought iron containers
They told me how much
          they admired
our local architecture for
          its grace
longevity and window boxes
of geranium on filigree
          balconies

I began to see it
          through new eyes

You'd been chatting
to a masculine woman
        with cropped hair
        I asked if you'd cheated
on me while I'd been away—
looking for an excuse
        to leave

When you said No, not really
I knew you had transgressed
in some small way   a kiss
        perhaps   not enough
to let me off the lead

A path had been created
through an avenue

of hardwood
to dead-end scrub

A girl with two dogs
was going there

Biting the Apple of Barnbougle

On the way to the Lost Farm
the strait is shallow   it's possible to fathom
the migration of souls and thylacines
something stirs it up out of the Heads—
a virgin glacier Mawson way, maybe

I am looking for phantoms of young black steer
dissolving in dunes, foraging in drifts of middens
when bumblebees the size of fairy wrens
swarm around my radiator looking for a piece
of real estate or dusting of errant pollen

Whop Whop   Looking up a chopper
flies a golf buggy over hand-planted marram
holding the north in place

At Paper Beach   lagoon and grove
so Game of Thrones in scape I expect Jon Snow
to row up in a Viking longship and start chipping
oysters off the conglomerates already gaping open
forced by a tern or grey gull with no pity

Somebody's been there
Somebody's always been there in places
you think pristine or impossible

Pademelons in varying stages of rot
a devil or two   spotted quolls squeezed flat
Smoke from the clear-felled
stacked like the dead along the Tamar

Without a City Wall

On the road to Ballarat
the argument thick between us
we take a wrong corner

Five bald hills bright white turbines
stand still like the crucifix waiting
for the infidel   Then one by one
from east to west, they turn, happy to earn
their keep, stop the speculation

Over the fence four lambs, not yet shorn
lie down
Across the field of fluoro canola
a pillar of smoke leans over

Silo Kick

In October when
canola competes
with young wheat

for Best in Show
white-faced boys
with Scottish names

compete with silos
that look like giant
clay pipes   *mirrool*

kicking footballs
over silos' mouths
Sometimes the silos

win   swallowing
the ball whole

Moomba as Iron Man Animé

Saturday night down Swanston Street
multitudes of teeny bat-boys grip black walls
grin with orphans' teeth   undo whole engines with filthy nails
As we look on   helpless

At the first crack   we are ***DOWN!***
Men in balaclavas   bullet-chokked men spray meat all over us
We joke about the regularity of it
Smelling like butchers Dying all over each other

Security officers –one a woman says the meat comes from us

       We are wafers   I tell her

Remembering lunch we turn the corner to heaven—
a tapas bar of white trans-angel boys
blonde this time bob-cut wigs narrow smiles again
hunched under the weight of those wings

One spots our muesli bars   offers us ham and bitter pickles
but what can we do with slabs of arse
from stalls where sows grow fat through iron bars? It's just too much

             We walk along the Yarra
                past newly arrived black swans
                  coiled and preening
                    away from the archipelago
                  of factory scum
                  vulnerable necks
                all five of them
              then step in turn
            on the cast iron sewer cap

Such symmetry   Such dirty beauty
Two empty beer cans lie apart on the grass like unhappy lovers
while Bulrush in a gang   Bulge from the undercroft
of the rattled bridge   like a Rape

The Roche Limit

Autumn becomes the colour of itself
        when through an open sash   a worry
of red dust on a tidal wave from the great
                artesian heart
fracked gibber stones glitter under our feet

        Is there no way out of it?

But no mosquitoes inside   Oh no
Their eyeballs turned lunar
under pressure of deep past

        Wands gear to water
        moved by the spell of spawn
        Malware spreading like a faith

If only the daddy of Fish Hideous
in the backyard eye of a pond had a tail
        he could rudder us

Instead   he's mutating in front of us
        fathering shoals of fry then fingerlings
with stumps   blotched with fungus, cancer, whatever

Our chickens moult furiously—
        one egg speckled and small

We don't eat embryos   yet
        Miracles have to start somewhere   a 3D printer?
and some do   love them

It must be the heat seeping in with the Ides

Bandanas cover our Munch mouths   our gasping lives and
the land   not quite fixed in our DNA   terrifies
        It's a Genet day

Cockroaches start clicking in the wattles
            then scatter unspeakably
under every slat of ply   antennae everywhere
            nuclear as an idea with a new name   Beware?

Free of the ice at last   slow death from multiple choice
        ubiquitous and forever
god knows   how long   spring

By the Divine Winds of January They Come

So many legs, closed wings
proceed in battalions
of what looks like self-determination
but isn't
Somehow they end up
in the laundry, in hallways
on soft backs
soft plates of armour useless
against white tiles, work boots

        What are they waiting for—
        for the world to turn a notch?

I urge them to retreat
but by morning
they've multiplied
lying completely still

        /like bowls and stone in that exhibition
        by dead-too-soon Akio Makigawa/

We vacuum or spray them
some days feeding them
in shovelfuls to the chickens
their little legs kick-kick
kicking against it
wings beat-beat-beating

        /like hearts of pre-flight
        man-boy kamikazes/

Oh Well it Must Be Autumn Then

We should have been stargazing from Moorabool
  but you were looking at me instead
    your eyes the nuclei of a supernova
      about to explode.
        My eyes became new
          in the gazing back at you.
Your hair was that blaze of canola
  stretching to the You Yangs—
    the one I look forward to every year.
      Some years it doesn't appear.
        Your lingo to explain dunes
          as lunettes, pivots, divots and giggions
            was impressive.
Some words I knew. Some you made up.
  I didn't care. You were marvellous.
    We sat on the pier to watch the night show.
      A man next to you said *Does she ever shut up?*
        You ignored him.
          He was a pig.
The night sky was pink
  like the pig sitting next to you—
    twinkly but hardly galaxy-dramatic
      the way I like it
        when the sky comes alive
          with dark matter cruising up and down
            like river-sharks looking for blood or love.
We waited inside
  for the mummers or masque.
    It was medieval anyway.
    It began with an M.
        Then we went to the Moat Ha!
          which was more like a lake

You were keen to see the bottom
    and toppled in at the last minute
        like a Mermaid/Man.
            I found you in a locker room
                no clothes on, flushed
                    a tissue in your teeth as peace offering
                        or invitation to tango.
I said I would go to the op shop
        to get you a new outfit but you already had
            a black skirt /cut on the bias/
                and red stilettos on by then.
                It no longer mattered.

We just were— pigless, genderless.
        Our last minutes together on earth. Glorious.

Live Love Long

on Monday nights pale grey men
hold me tight to demonstrate
the ins and outs of the
cha cha cha

on Tuesday I plant banksia
integrifolia to lure the trembling
spinebill to new nectar in the
neighbourhood

(by the way) the snail has a brain
is a bit of a Don Juan when it comes to love
sleeps through the cold   drought
or flood   could be your
teenage son   then Venus all eyes
sees lovers entwine super-coiled in courtship
before the love dart shoots home

then they smoke a cigarette   go for a piss
just a story   random spiral
unravelling in a soft shoe shuffle
hip hop freestyle
a slow slow quickquick   slow

Expresh v Colonial Landscape

He's too hot to touch   in bed after midnight
batteries chokked from the charge of the day

        Painted his years in the way of von Guérard
monster canvas   little leaves   shady detail   in his
felt-funny hat
        He's crag-man with scalpel on the lookout
for the next big commish   big wheels spitting
rev-rev-revving   three-point perspective
        in a Baroquish frame

Her days are broad-brushed in the gloom of a Rothko
wall-papery   covering cracks
the worry of a Tucker   fug of a Turner
        blinding hangover   too many men   cigarettes
In younger days Hester melancholic
they said she had a wide aorta
        blood poured over her gunmetal carpet
turning it black   Impatiens petals splatter
    white tiles think American Beauty
        don't think Pro Hart

Yet side by side
    at the end of each day
        they say 'Had a good one?'
            and watch Deal or no Deal
                before the Six o' Clock News

Vagina Dentata

Sag, Snake, Swallet, Swallow…

How do they avoid it-this heavenly pit lurking beneath
desire paths?
Breeding ewes cluster as they lamb and wool
but they don't fall in.

Divers canoe the limestone yawn,
drop to John Deere harvesters, bull skulls and barbed wire
slung down this marvellous hole.

Some take time out from iPhones to bask like wobbegongs.
Young soldiers—finned and slippery, nose into tunnels
where algae /*moss-to-be*/ nibbles patiently, biding its time.

They are lulled.

Sinister minerals from this portal make a womb
fit for a platoon.

Horses put hooves through the green veneer.
A thousand tonnes of rubble make no plug in it.
Boys who would be men drown in it,
knowing it's there.

Landscape/ Portrait Dilemma in Taking a Selfie

To create an algorithm that measures beauty—compose,
illuminate, expose
> *or fill the birdbath for firetails descending*
> *when heat goes out of the sun*

Use human annotations to classify emotional polarity of
each image
> *or stroke the backbone of a young fern*
> *spooling from the under-storey*

Whether positive or negative assess originality compared to
others
> *or say sorry to the old wattle,*
> *sap bleeding out through torn skin*

Race, gender and age are largely uncorrelated with
photographic beauty
> *so situate blue salvia next to desert gaura*
> *and white iris as in a Monet*

Females are more memorable, brighter and post-processed
> *Colour hangs in the heart*

Aesthetic score relates to sharpness of facial landmarks
> *The promise of a river*

Men smile less than women
> *at the end or beginning of a journey*

A common or garden point-and-shoot has this facility inbuilt
> *Smile*

When the Light Fails

Thylacine

I saw you, I did.
You crossed in front of me
at midnight on the Fish Creek Road.
You were dead skinny with a
bone of a tail.

I was driving
in my canary yellow Corolla
with my young lover in the dead of night.
A dead secret between us, Foxy Boy.
Remember me?

Kathy K

she milks twelve cows in the bare-arsed raw,
pays the plumber's bill with a grimy fuck
on tie-dyed sheets
breeds two stud boys to *'see how it feels'*
and with the delicate hands
of an aristocrat gathers her hair into a comb

driving home alone through ghost gums
4am out of Castlemaine
her foxy dog catches the whiff of
kebab wrapper under the accelerator and
with the reflex of a hunter short
on thrills, leaps into a role play

she tries to brake, takes the bend too fast
and whacks into the nearest tree
it's legend for Miss Bush Tragedy and
in the words of someone not close,
I don't believe that story about the dog,
I think she was pissed.

and now she stands there, and not there
in the same crepe dress
cherokee hair, terracotta skin.
There's something jarring between you and I,
                              says the Lady K.
You're dead, I say
but from the next room
I hear her sigh.

Hollows.org

a man remembered in a whale of a rock
half smooth   half rough
names and dates hard to see
on this slant of granite mammal
his last joke perhaps
Fred Cossom Hollows
big name in the Bourke cemetery
turn left at the gate

Ingrained

They lived on the flats of Nhill
the old woman will tell you

She's seen the eyes of shop fronts glaze over,
vacant on the day we drove through
in our hybrid cars in matched silence

She swears on her mother's grave
young wheat turned bare soil green
silos cracked with grain in good years
flowing over in low mountain ranges
tarped in white canvas, kept dry

She's seen the creek run wild,
then collapse again

And she says   *Let me tell you how we lived*
How the dead stay alive in the mind

Down the main street   the Salvos' mannequin
hands on hips under a beach umbrella

A pyramid of dead men's clothes saturated
by a rare shower   limbs spilling over the sides

This is my town, the old woman says
This is her man and his John Deere

Look!   *Everything's for sale*

An Hour in the Gallery of Glass

What to do   in the space left ahead
Is it enough to wander through a forest of glass
past paling fences incised with lines of an old woman
            who might give her secrets away?

A tree of wire grows out of a rusted wheel hub
Ears of wheat sprout artfully from
corrugations
                        Is this what we have become
                        How we manage the past
                        Make it beautiful
                        or leave it buckling among salt bush
                        and clots of granite
                        as testament to survival?

What to do with the space left inside —
            the glass heart   blue faces
etched somehow into ventricles
and that lotus flower   such resilience
held by   an arcing stem   an aorta almost
                        unbreakable   dry eye open to the monsoon
where cumuli assemble
then disperse as those forced to flee
                        across the diaspora

How they must ponder liquid light
in an alien sky   the way sand forms
in lunettes and sings of the lost
            and found   the urgency of precipitation —
            the next fall

Lynx Rufous

When I saw you shape-shift
from wild cat to kestrel
riding thermals over the Wimmera
you were trailing cloud vapour
mouth in a chaste kiss
clothed in the angel calm
of plainest cotton off-white
& would have smiled feline
at the cliché

Only then could I forgive you
the rope
slung over the bedroom door
tough enough to take
our frail bone-weight

Forgive you for the time you wrote

*I wonder what it would have been like
if we'd been together*

When the Moon Says it's Okay

I broke your heart you said. I've known a lot of broken
hearts and some ended worse than others. A broken heart
is a true thing. And it's not just us. Animals die of broken
hearts. Even frogs have personalities. My friend has two
tree frogs and one is a real standoffish little bastard.

But to die of a broken heart seems such a sad affair; like my
mate who had a bad night, and once he'd packed his skis;
The Notebook for God's sake, and a photo album of him
looking good in flares for someone with red hair, tied a
rope to the handle of his bedroom door. He had an ensuite,
an exposed brick wall, and strung himself up like those
cows in the abattoirs with the big eyes and confused looks,
the *I can't believe this shit* look in their bodies; yawing and
fighting and stretching to get up and eat that grass; and
only lying down when the desert sun slips under the edge
and the moon says *It's okay.*

Searching for Mirage Girl Explorer

You took the path of gibber rock
from Port Augusta to Uluru
where time folds in and on itself
placed it in chunks
in your large pockets.
Dreamer, flaneur— the desert
is littered with your shoes.

They have a special name for you—
Kuti—beautiful swan.
I come across reflections
in pools created to guide
the wayfarer—an inch deep in places,
unfathomable in others.
Still I cannot find you.

Sand flats of Kati Thanda
terrify—their salty endlessness.
Once you appeared
when the light began to waver.
I thought I saw you tossed
in an open coracle with a calico sail,
a hand-held compass set north.

Mungerannie

Sand flats and salt bush
mean nothing to us

yet in this sparseness
I marvel at the repetition

the clinging on
and the way I manufacture

kindness in needle bushes
parasols against the sun

Some days I could get used to
leaving tracks like wild dogs

an emu and his
chicks, a stumpy or a snake

Once I sailed Cooper Creek
on a flatbed ferry

this time I blow the top layer
off the gibber plain

in a truck   But we have arrived!
invading homes of spitfire birds

the intrigue of a lizard slide
At dusk jibber-jabber

up and down a tonal ladder
Always the urgency of a parrot

Gnats have started their
corroboree in a column of sunshine

before switching down
while a black snake effortlessly

lifts itself from the neck
of the gas bottle like a symbol

Dingo Girl

Safe inside your canvas dreaming
       of the red track westward across the dunes

the lean shape-shifter   toes of a dancer
       foxtrots the fringe   Camp follower

nose to the north   she takes the shape of
       a desert grass   spinifex dry
same pale yellow   same drift as the wind

It's then you daub the ochre
       white for the star in the eye   Insinuate
a dark shadow   minimal   abstract perhaps

Next morning the palette licked clean

Painting Rock Woman Uluru

We snake around her stubborn hulk
pat the sacred skin   scaled as a desert skink
a red brick wall

Crawl into her hydra mouths   leave footprints
on her tongue with Blundstones
and white runners

She's winky round the eyes
a kewpie doll pitted with acne
on a fresh cheek

Memorial plaques are stapled
to her thighs   Marcia Brian Leslie
George have toppled off these
ancestral slopes   *fulfilling lifelong
ambition*   ignoring the warning

Ants like us don't creep over her curves today
Clouds party with grey haze from Alice fires
It's windy as hell   the rains have come

Frogs clack-clack love calls like music sticks
before the dry sets them hard in red again

For now a weeping wet folds a shroud
or bridal veil   a skull tattooed into her back
spinifex sprouts in her sorry cuts

Under wide skirts a kindergarten of baby river gums
wild flowers   sweet as a newborn's fingernails
charm us with their pinks, yellows

At sunset she will pose for greedy eyes
we steal her stories, trawling reservoirs
for sorrow Ghosts swirl about this cathedral

jelly baby dugong dreaming
nose of dolphin caterpillar
grungy steampunk armadillo

We make her ours

Heysen's Ranges

whisper from
barrows of the dead

So much mess
        and melancholy
in tired sandstone
north of the Goyder Line

We sprawl across claypans, salt stretch
        the falling away

        and as we cross Emu, Leigh
        and every other dry creek
        railway sleepers

        nudged over
        the batter of the Ghan
        are totems

        We gather then burn them
        devouring
        our dubious history

Farina Farina

Stone ruins on the Ghan kindle
the dream of being a Kidman or Durack
scanning the flat for a castle   some green

We fossick for nails   find a bean tin rusted
through   gibber stone to fit a young man's
hand a thousand years ago   big enough
to shock a skink into the next life

In the cemetery cameleers face east
next to the oasis for new nomads
where polished Jayco caravans
boast hot and cold running water

Facing west   the shell of a Holden
nudges the corrugated lean of a water tank
Pale weeds hide and seek where wheels
once turned to Lake Eyre in the rain
for a picnic or a stolen kiss

We snap the blue through a window
with no glass   frame of a shifting
canvas   In a wide, sharp sky there's
the melancholy hush   Light breeze blows
spinifex through the bones   of this town

Lizards of Leigh Creek

The bluey on the concrete step
unfurls his clover-leafed tongue
and when I move close
I hear a faint hiss
but he seems harmless enough

and when I poke out my pink tongue
he seems to laugh and turn
            on his stumpy tail
the spitting image without the eyes
no mouth   perfectly angled feet

            I couldn't see the point
            of such camouflage on the town's pet reptile
when I saw his brother squashed
under the wheel of an SUV on our way out

while his ancestor mother
a ribbon of rock across the gibber plain
lay in her silica bed
            in mourning

We passed her
            west of the Oodnadatta track

In Flagrante Delicto

As we witnessed her worldly goods
craned to the back of a truck
        we lost count of big-eyed babushkas,
        earth-bound cushions,
        empty frames waiting for a thought.

She was poised under the eaves of heaven
brushing swallows from her hair
        chain-smoking Gitanes
        a bottle of St Emilion at her winged feet
        as Japanese masks of a couple

        /he with a cracked cheek
        from being dropped in '87/

        made their chalk-faced way
        to the mountain.

Ravines formed by boxes of books
        gave off the smell of old forests,
        dry rivers, death in the Gulag,
        death on the land, dead ideas
        like truth and adjectives.

And the tribal rug she'd rolled on
        over centuries making babies.

We can see it
        in the failing light
        stained by blood and love.

Her Face

He trowels ghostly white
rude hero of the canvas

each daub a paragraph
of her smudged story

slapped into life   oil on
coarse linen she is quilt-cosy

in collusion   surprise
collides in every stroke

Slow Death of a Cockatoo

the glass bird   /fragile, quiet/
abandoned   by the gang
          puts all her colour
                  /sulphur /
into one last push
          as if nibbling twigs
could prolong it

up the crackling bark
      of an ancient pine
                  she yaws
wings tucked in
                  worried by crow
intent on eye   coming in
              bouncing

          after a worried while
I drive off in low gear
          as if that might slow
it down   /this melancholy tableau/
toward low hills
              punctuated by
                  flysch sediments
swallowing
          a surrendering sun

Allegro non Troppo That's What it Triggered

Late morning travelling
south of Capricornia
through the dull interior
of infinite bitumen
you could lose
the will to live if it weren't
for the show on high

An archipelago of behemoths
is lugging at the speed of cloud
across the screen
Duck on a wall   blind snail
splayed-leg toad
They seem in a parade
en route to some celestial ark
Noah letting them all in

By dusk the light
is a descending grey
wan tones from the failing sun
and in a whisper of sweepers
a turtle with no flippers
turns into gossamer wings

Amputation by godly brushstroke
True nature of cirrus

Cassowary

Up early in our rented Getz
brightly red   pokey on the turns
we cross a Myall Creek   there must be two

Not this one   New South Wales 1838
when thirty Wirrayaraay mums
and bubs   old guys whittling sticks
are bushwhacked into a stockyard

scorched one by one   behind a hill
making barbecue   young gin for dessert
tasty treat for hard-working stockmen

But this one   sleepy Daintree spot
the foot of Mt Sorrow   PK's Jungle Bar where
we drink beer   watch the Ashes disappear
into the new Sony flatscreen

Heading south we stop to let
a cassowary dad
and fluffy dino babe
walk out to peck the bitumen
road kill remains

Like the boy section D row 7
of the Port cemetery
slashed to the bowel by that
middle toe   stabbed
by raptor stiletto
Aged sixteen   Dan Mclean
pupil no 4
caught in the creek
learning his last lesson

Our cameras focus on the neck
cobalt blue   scarlet wattle

Black gloss of forest demon
trapped in a Canon click
So easy through the lens

Relics from the Forest of the Gonds

I'd read that continents had been joined
          before ice and the big thaw
& wanted to see what I could find

I found a pair of green shoes
              gender indeterminate
a pigeon pair kissing at the instep
          left in front of right
toes at five to one in a still life

They seemed on the verge of setting off
backdrop a scribble of leaf and pod
blown beachward by an easterly

It made an attractive canvas   abstract
the way I like it

I looked around   I was alone
with black tongues and curved throat lines
          eyelets laced in a figure of eight
          a pair of green shoes, barely worn
placed carefully by a careful person

Had they been left for me or
had someone walked into a sea of box jellyfish
          to a painful death
          it was the hot season after all

A needle of casuarina was stitching a story
sand already forming drifts
              on the south face

Gondwana the Betrothed

When we are no longer married
to frozen lands of the south
as we nudge north to Pacific archipelagos
coral and scaly vertebrates, edible sunsets

and pawpaw for breakfast we will settle
briefly next to ancient reefs of strontium.
Polyps of anemone three million years young
will bloom in a crinkled zone.

It will be a case of old against new
gently rubbing one against the other in a forced
but not wholly unexpected or unwelcome union.

One day we will meet again
and once welded together
birth new ruched peaks.

These will be good for watchtowers
intrepid trackers making their way to the deep
looking for signs of the long gone
that when found will be timid
in hiding behind palm or tendril of wild vine.

    Reconnected at last
    we will snuggle up
    with our new mate
    for good, or at least
    for a very long time.

Notes/Inspirations

Solastalgia in the Mouth of the Great Vowel Shift—
New Zealand wattle bird, the Huia, not seen since 1909 and a recording of its call made in 1949 by Henare Hemana.
Bird of—*'Bird of Paradise' by Margaret Preston, 1925.*
Leopard Day—*lines by Pascale Petit.*
The Life of Trees and the Childless—
'The Hidden Life of Trees', What They Feel, How They Communicate - Discoveries from a Secret World by Peter Wohlleben.
Emoto's Theory of Rock Pool Phenomena—*Dr. Masaru Emoto 1943-2014, believed water could react to positive thoughts and polluted water could be cleaned through prayer and positive visualisation.*
Shark Baby Hallelujah—*Mr Finch, UK based sculptor using natural fabrics.*
He Makes a Difficult Choice
Australian scientist, David Goodall, travelled to Switzerland to end his own life, legally, on May 10, 2018. Rachel Funari disappeared on Bruny Island in 2011.
Little Picture—*Sara Watt, Australian film maker, 1958-2011*
How Deep is Your Love—*The Children's Tree —Ficus Macrophylla—Moreton Bay Fig in Sydney Royal Botanical Gardens.*
Moomba as Iron Man Animé—*'Humours of an Election' by William Hogarth.*
Vagina Dentata—*Kilsby's Sinkhole, South Australia.*
Landscape/Portrait Dilemma in Taking a Selfie—
John R Neeson—River Bend Installation.
Ingrained—*Lines by Brian Turner, Kirkuk Oilfield 1927.*
Silo Kick—*Mirrool, name of a town in the Riverina. Mirrool— a word meaning clay pipe in early languages.*
Searching for Mirage Girl Explorer—*im Kelly Theobald, writer, jillaroo, died on the Birdsville Track in 2017.*
Cassowary—*In 1838 white settlers murdered 28 Wirrayaraay men, women and children near Myall Creek Station, NSW. The perpetrators were the first to be tried and hanged for such an atrocity.*

In Flagrante Delicto—*im Mirka Mora 1928-2018.*
Her Face—*Ben Quilty's portrait of Margaret Olley, winner of the Archibald Prize, 2011.*

Acknowledgements

I would like to acknowledge the traditional owners of Country, the lands, seas, waterways, skyscapes and histories that inspired much of this work, in particular, the land of the Wadawurrung where I am settled, for now.

I would like to thank the editors of the following publications where the poems first appeared, some in earlier versions:

Australian Poetry Journal, The Best Australian Poetry (UQP), The Blue Nib, Cordite Review, Cumquat, Envoi, ETZ, foam:e, fourW30 New Writing, Gangway (Austria), 'Tango Boleo', 'Mirage' and 'Unsettled' (Pocket Books, Ginninderra Press), Ink Sweat and Tears, Island, Not Very Quiet, New Walk Magazine, Obsessed with Pipework, Overland, Plumwood Mountain, Poetry Salzburg (Austria) Rabbit Poetry, Red Room 'New Shoots' Anthology, Shearsman, Southerly, Stylus, Ofi Press (Mexico), The Journal, The Lake, Under the Radar, Unusual Work, Wet Ink, Windmills.

'The Roche Limit' and *'A Minute Past Dawn'* were highly commended in the WB Yeats Poetry Prize 2018.
'How Deep is Your Love' was shortlisted for *Red Room's New Shoots Poetry Prize,* 2017.
'41 North 50 West' won *Best Poem, Booranga Writers four W New Writing,* 2016.
'The Secret Life of Trees and the Childless' was longlisted for *The Rialto Nature and Place Prize, UK,* 2016.
'Live Love Long' won the *National Tango Poetry Prize,* 2014.

I would also like to acknowledge Владимир Мельник, Dnipro, Ukraine for permission to use 'Woman with Suitcase' as cover image for *Eye*.

Bio

Julie Maclean fell in love with Australian marsupials around the age of six. As a teacher of English, Dance and Drama and fed up with British politics and class, she arrived in Melbourne from the UK in 1976, aged 24, with a suitcase and $300. *'Eye'* is her second full collection; a chronicle of her travels around the continent she dreamed of as a child.

Her first collection, *'When I Saw Jimi'* was published as joint winner of the *Geoff Stevens Memorial Poetry Prize,* Indigo Dreams, UK, 2014. As a memoir of growing up in Sixties' Britain, the full manuscript was shortlisted for *The Crashaw Prize,* Salt. She is the author of eight pamphlets including an exploration of Scandi Noir, *'Kiss of the Viking'* (Poetry Salzburg). As joint winner of the *Dreich Slims Poetry Competition, 'was red was love'* was published in 2024. She lives on the Surf Coast, Wadawurrung country, Victoria.